WEIGHED IN THE BALANCE AND FOUND WANTING

THE FAILURE OF PUBLIC SCHOOLS
THE NEED FOR CHRISTIAN EDUCATION

(REVISED EDITION)

CHRISTIAN LIBERTY PRESS

1996

Copyright © 1996 by Christian Liberty Press
Printing 2007

All rights reserved. No part of this book may be reproduced or transmitted in any form or by any means, electronic or mechanical, without written permission from the publisher. Brief quotations embodied in critical articles or reviews are permitted.

A publication of
Christian Liberty Press
502 West Euclid Avenue
Arlington Heights, Illinois 60004
www.christianlibertypress.com

ISBN 978-1-930367-75-3
1-930367-75-9

Cover design by Eric D. Bristley
Layout Edward J. Shewan

Printed in the United States of America

Contents

Chapter		Pages
	Introduction	*v*
1	Students At Risk	1–14
2	Parental Reasons For Leaving Public Education	15–31
3	A Time For Change	32-34

INTRODUCTION

John Dewey, known as the father of progressive education, signed the infamous Humanist Manifesto. So did D. F. Potter, the author of *Humanism: A New Religion*. In his book Potter writes that "education is thus a most powerful ally of humanism, and every American public school is a school of humanism. What can the theistic Sunday schools, meeting for an hour once a week, and teaching only a fraction of the children, do to stem the tide of a five-day program of humanistic teaching?"

In wrestling with that question back in the 1960s I came to the conclusion that government-controlled education is not the answer—and that Sunday schools, Awana Clubs, church youth groups, and Sunday services can never offset a five-day-a-week, and six-to-seven-hour-a-day exposure to humanistic instruction. There must be an alternative!

And yes, there is a biblical answer. It is consistent Christian education. Because of this we organized the independent and non-denominational Christian Liberty Academy in 1968, and our home-schooling program, CLASS, in 1969. God has blessed us with tens of thousands of students ... and families across America and around the world have been blessed as children have been trained in the way they should go.

I am thankful to a home school mother (name unknown) who many years ago sent me information which has been edited, revised, and/or rewritten, and expanded. It has been included in chapter two. I have collected, researched, and prepared materials to provide you with an acute analysis of the present educational crisis. My thanks to all who have assisted in this project.

Dr. Paul D. Lindstrom
1939–2002

CHAPTER 1

STUDENTS AT RISK

Times have certainly changed! Just ask the folks in Fresno, California. Increasing attendance at the local public school brings in more money for the school district. State funding is based on average daily attendance. How, therefore, do you get students to class more often? Here's one experiment. Fresno High School bet $10,000 of tax-payer funds that prizes of cash and merchandise would bring students to class on time and more often. The school started an attendance lottery. Weekly prizes were small—a portable stereo, for instance. But prizes at the end of each quarter were as large as home stereos, video cassette recorders, and $200 in cash. Fresno High's school site council, administrators, and student council approved the plan. Fifty-four teachers agreed with the idea, and eleven did not. Needless to say, the plan was an educational failure.

Of all of the problems facing the United States today, many thoughtful persons believe the decay in education to be the most important. It is less spectacular than the economy, or the Middle East, or scandals in government and so on, and it receives comparatively less publicity from the media. It is, nonetheless, the most ominous because, by a combination of insidious design and sheer ineptitude, it is turning out young citizens, the nation of tomorrow, who are almost totally unprepared to face life, intellectually and spiritually. To further abuse a much-abused quotation: "A little learning is a dangerous thing."

WHAT ABOUT READING?

Protagonists of modern education will rise immediately and demand by what right can one call education "decaying"? Well, take reading for example. To most of us, the simple ability to read is as natural as breathing. From the Greeks through the early Americans, reading was recognized as a necessity, even if education progressed no further. Recently, three major employers in the largest midwestern city, the telephone and electric companies and a giant oil corporation, admitted that they had to set up "schools" within their own organizations so that recently graduated high school students could be taught to read well enough to be able to understand some part of their new jobs! Parenthetically, the school budget for that city is almost half again as large as the total United States budget for any year up to 1918 (and that was a war year)!

Before the draft was discontinued, an officer involved in its planning operations wrote, "[The draftees'] performance in the relatively undemanding Armed Forces Qualification Test revealed that they are too unlettered to read and understand even the simplest Army training manuals." Things have now gone from bad to worse.

A former member of the U.S. Senate, a semanticist and educator before his election, wrote that only one or two members of that world-changing body had sufficient command of the English language to use it correctly. He continued, "A large and growing number of children in this country are being given only a token education, a sham and a fraud."

A Nation At Risk is an unbelievable report on educational life in America. It is an official U.S. government document. As the years have passed since the National Commission on Excellence in Education first published its findings in 1983, the crisis has only worsened. The report noted:

> "If an unfriendly foreign power had attempted to impose on America the mediocre educational performance that exists today, we might well have viewed it as an act of war. As it stands, we have allowed this to happen to ourselves.... We have, in effect, been committing an act of unthinking, unilateral educational disarmament.
>
> "Our society and its educational institutions seem to have lost sight of the basic purposes of schooling.... The educational foundations of our society are presently being eroded by a rising tide of mediocrity that threatens our very future as a nation and a people."

The educational dimensions of the risk were amply documented in testimony received by the Commission. For example:

> "International comparisons of student achievement, completed a decade ago, reveal that on 19 academic tests American students were

never first or second and, in comparison with other industrialized nations, were last seven times.

"Tens of millions of American adults are functionally illiterate by the simplest tests of everyday reading, writing, and comprehension.

"About 13 percent of all 17-year-olds in the United States can be considered functionally illiterate. Functional illiteracy among minority youth may run as high as 40 percent.

"Average achievement of high school students on most standardized tests is now lower than 26 years ago when Sputnik was launched.

"Over half the population of gifted students do not match their tested ability with comparable achievement in school.

"The College Board's Scholastic Aptitude Tests (SAT) demonstrate a virtually unbroken decline. Average verbal scores fell over 50 points and average mathematics scores dropped nearly 40 points.

"College Board achievement tests also reveal consistent declines in recent years in such subjects as physics and English.

"Both the number and proportion of students demonstrating superior achievement on the SATs (i.e., those with scores of 650 or higher) have also dramatically declined.

"Many 17-year-olds do not possess the "higher order" intellectual skills we should expect of them. Nearly 40 percent cannot draw inferences from written material; only one-fifth can write a persuasive essay; and only one-third can solve a mathematics problem requiring several steps.

"There was a steady decline in science achievement scores of U.S. 17-year-olds as measured by national assessments of science.

"Remedial mathematics courses in public 4-year colleges increased by 72 percent and now constitute one-quarter of all mathematics courses taught in those institutions.

"Average tested achievement of students graduating from college is also lower.

"Business and military leaders complain that they are required to spend millions of dollars on costly remedial education and training programs in such basic skills as reading, writing, spelling, and computation. The

Department of the Navy, for example, reported to the Commission that one-quarter of its recent recruits cannot read at the ninth grade level, the minimum needed simply to understand written safety instructions. Without remedial work they cannot even begin, much less complete, the sophisticated training essential in much of the modern military.

The report therefore went on to say, "*The average graduate* of our schools and colleges today is not as well-educated as the average graduate of 25 or 35 years ago, when a much smaller proportion of our population completed high school and college. The negative impact of this fact likewise cannot be overstated."

HELPLESS AND HOPELESS

The results of the most comprehensive literacy study ever undertaken by the U.S. Department of Education were released in 1993. The 14 million dollar project revealed that nearly half of all adult Americans cannot read and write sufficiently to get and keep a decent job. More than half of all high school graduates were found to have restricted abilities in math and reading. This, and even more unbelievable educational information, was widely disseminated by the news media in September, 1993 (*Boston Globe*, 9/19/93; *USA Today*, 9/9/93; *Chicago Sun Times*, 9/27/93).

An article in one of our local newspapers is entitled "The Real Horror of Being Illiterate." It begins, "It is virtually impossible for those Americans who have beaten the system to comprehend the full horror of not being able to read. Non-readers flounder and fall back, they become the drop-outs, the pushed-outs, the unemployed and the unemployable—frustrated and bitter, helpless and hopeless. Not for them the pleasure of reading great American and English literature. Not for them the relaxation of the sports pages, or the humor of the comics. Their lives are void inside a vacuum. All too tragically they are often considered mentally retarded." The author continues, "The evidence is overwhelming that millions of junior high and high school students today cannot read their textbooks. Millions more stumble and struggle their way through." Yes, it certainly must be said that the government educational system is a sick, multi-billion dollar social institution in the midst of a crisis.

Parents on the Warpath

I have in front of me two issues of the *Readers Digest Magazine*. In one there is an article by the title, "Are We Becoming A Nation Of Illiterates?" The other issue begins with the story, "Why Johnny Can't Write." These are most interesting articles. They point out that parents all over the United States are disturbed. They are disturbed because children are not being taught to read, write, spell, and do math as they should be taught. Millions of parents throughout the United States are upset not only with their children's academic deficiencies, but with all of the amoral sex education, socialism, sensitivity training, value's clarification, behavior modification, drugs, violence, outcome-based education, the lack of discipline and many other things within the government schools. Parents are disturbed that in the government schools Christian ideals and principles are simply not being taught. Old fashioned morality has been thrown right out the school window. No wonder parents are upset. No wonder they are removing their children from the government schools.

General Nathan F. Twining, on his retirement as Chairman of the Joint Chiefs of Staff, stated, "I can't help but wish that our educational processes had inspired a stronger faith in American values, and the resolution and the guts and fortitude to maintain them." Statistics and comments abound. Perhaps they are summed up by the cynical remark of one critic, "Johnny may not read; but, he can be so well-adjusted that he won't know the difference."

However, to John Dewey, one of the modern founders of progressive education, and his cohorts, the purpose of education was to adjust the individual to life. In other words, education for education's sake was worthless. Its value lay in reducing the individual to the common level of his "peer group." No educational competitiveness, no grading, and no discipline would be the ideal. This era saw the beginning of such terms as "orientation," "group dynamics," "social living," "peer groups," et al.

A Look at the Past

Historians (merely chronicling the development of education without delving into the reasons for its transitions) have almost uniformly ascribed the immense rise of the concepts of progressive education to the increasing dissatisfaction with nineteenth-century classicism. The foundation was actually laid many years earlier, however. Progressive education was the result of a carefully managed, very long-term program.

Education was regarded as of primary importance by the American colonists. "Prior to the introduction of compulsory public education," one historian has noted, "Americans were probably the most literate people in the world." Almost all of this literacy resulted from private schooling—either home schooling or in traditional schools. There was no government interference. To quote the same author again, "There were no accrediting agencies, no regulatory boards, no teacher certification requirements. Parents had the freedom to choose whatever kind of school or education they wanted for their children." Traditional private schooling did not preclude the poor. Almost every school had provisions for charity pupils. Pennsylvania actually paid the tuition to a private school for parents who could not afford to do so.

Thus, the "common school" (as the first public schools were called) did not come into existence because education was offered only to the wealthy, as some progressive educators would like us to believe. Common schools were created in response to a need. They appeared first in Massachusetts to insure the transfer of Christianity to succeeding generations. The Reformation had established the authority of the Bible, and its proper interpretation required a high degree of specific literacy. Hence, communities of a certain size required elementary schools, and larger communities grammar schools, so that Latin, Greek, and Hebrew could be taught for the proper appreciation of Biblical literature. These common schools were purely local. There was no state or central authority. The consolidating link was biblical Christianity. However, private schools and home schooling continued to flourish, being preferred by most citizens.

THE BIG LIE

For a number of years there was "peaceful coexistence." By the 1820's Boston had become quite a city, and a quietly determined group of state school advocates began to stir up trouble by pointing out how many children were not in school, how this bred crime and poverty, and how the compulsory schooling statutes must be sternly enforced.

Samuel L. Blumenfeld, a good friend and educator-historian whom I quoted earlier, has, by diligent research, managed to give statistical lie to these pronouncements. At the time in question, there were 2,360 pupils enrolled in public schools, more than 4,000 in private schools, and only 243 of the children over seven years of age were not in school. In other words, less than 5% of the children of Boston did not attend school. Many of these children were probably being home schooled.

The proponents of state control were loud and clear, however. As happens every day in our times, a small noisy group succeeds in making a mount out of molehill. This group was greatly assisted by the great increase in Unitarianism, which vigorously contested biblical Christianity and managed to gain control (intellectually and spiritually) of Harvard, the former bastion of true Christian beliefs. The Unitarians thought that man was not basically sinful, but quite capable of perfecting himself. Therefore, since God was a rather disinterested Being, it behooved the Unitarians to help man to perfect himself ... by public education.

Great impetus was given to this movement by a Scotsman named Robert Owen, who believed that a man's character is largely determined by his environment. To prove his theories, Owen set up a totally socialist community in New Harmony, Indiana, shortly after 1825. New Harmony failed miserably in a matter of two years, but this only goaded Owen further. People were not ready for this type of socialistic existence, he decided, because they had not been properly educated. Therefore, they must be educated into socialism.

As the nineteenth century wore on, the Christian faith diminished in strength, and the new "rational man" concept assumed greater importance. The greatest single stimulus to this, intellectually, was the work of Georg Friederich Hegel, a German philosopher who promulgated the idea that man was potentially god-like, capable of creating unlimited good.

This, of course, was great ammunition for the Unitarians. At about the same time, in the 1820's, they "discovered" the Prussian school system—a regimented, structured operation, completely controlled by the state. A French philosopher, whom it was fashionable to admire, espoused these concepts, and added more publicity.

The Laboring Mann

Thus, the stage was set for the appearance of Horace Mann, the father of state education. Unfortunately, he was singularly capable and devoted to his cause to a point of virtual fanaticism. Under his guidance, the movement grew prodigiously.

A further major step was the creation of the first state normal school: to teach teachers what (not how) to teach. This takeover took time, and there was much opposition; but the latter was ineffectual because it was not organized, much the same situation we find ourselves in today.

In 1825, an opponent of state controlled education, James Carter, said that public education was "an engine to sway the public sentiment, the public morals, and the public religion, more powerful than any other in the possession of government."

It wasn't until 1834 and the "Free School Act" that any state could tax for school purposes. By 1837, Horace Mann and the Harvard Unitarians had succeeded in enacting state legislation to remake Massachusetts's public school system in the centralized Prussian image. Other states soon followed suit. This was the beginning of socialized (government) education and poor education.

Historically discerning Christians noted the impossibility of the professed neutrality of public secular education. One such man was Professor A. A. Hodge of Princeton Theological Seminary. He stated in 1887:

> "I am as sure as I am of Christ's reign that a comprehensive and centralized system of national education, separated from religion, as is commonly proposed, will prove the most appalling engine for the

propagation of anti-Christian and atheistic unbelief ... which this sin-rent world has ever seen. The tendency is to hold that the system must be altogether secular ... that the education provided by the common government should be entirely emptied of all religious character.... It is capable of exact demonstration that if every party in the State has the right of excluding from the public schools whatever he does not believe to be true, then he that believes most must give way to him who believes absolutely nothing, no matter in how small a minority the atheists or the agnostics may be. It is self evident that on this scheme, if it is consistently and persistently carried out in all parts of the country, the United States system of national popular education will be the most efficient and wide instrument for the propagation of atheism which the world has ever seen."

R. J. Rushdoony, in his book, *The Nature of the American System*, says of Horace Mann, "First and foremost, Mann was a Unitarian. New England Unitarianism was in the forefront of the battle for state education. For Mann, Unitarianism was true Christianity, and, with humorless zeal, he fought for his holy faith." Rushdoony continues, "Mann labored, therefore, to free the schools from their basically Christian and independent nature in order to give them true direction, as he saw it, in terms of the state. His hostility against Calvinism and against the free schools of his day was bitter and intense."

ONE PIECE AT A TIME

Let me add another piece to the puzzle. I am quoting from *NEA: Trojan Horse In American Education*, written by Samuel L. Blumenfeld:

> "While Thorndike developed and formulated the psychological basis for progressive education, John Dewey formulated its social aims. Dewey joined the faculty at Columbia in 1904, as a professor of philosophy. In 1884, he had gone from Johns Hopkins to the University of Michigan and, in 1894, to the University of Chicago, as head of the department of philosophy, psychology and education. It was there, in 1886, that Dewey created the famous Laboratory School, which was to be for his department what a lab is for a biology or chemistry department.

"Dewey wanted to test certain philosophical and psychological ideas in practical application with real live children, and a laboratory school was the best place in which to do it. As with so many liberal intellectuals who had abandoned Christianity, Dewey's philosophy had evolved from Hegelian idealism to socialist materialism. The purpose of the school was to show experimentally how education could be reformed to create little socialists instead of little capitalists who, in the long run, would change the American economic system."

Listen to the words of John Dewey, whose philosophy is the "backbone" of our public education system:

"There is no God and there is no soul. Hence, there are no needs for the props of traditional religion. With dogma and creed excluded, then immutable truth is also dead and buried. There is no room for fixed, natural law or moral absolutes."

You could have taken those words right out of the mouth of Karl Marx! Little wonder that the Dewey-ite secular humanists who have led education in this country for the past seventy years have helped to produce a veritable slime pit of immorality, drug addiction, sexual perversion, permissiveness, and, as the National Commission on Education reported, a nation of growing ignorance.

NEA Madness

To really understand, however, the transformation of American education, we must understand the organization that began reaching for monopoly control over education from its inception. I am talking now about the National Education Association—the NEA. It was the NEA that became the driving force behind John Dewey's so-called progressive education.

In a 1972 NEA handbook, NEA President Morrison says,

"The NEA started in 1856 with an organization called the National Teachers Association. At the first meeting in Philadelphia, it was suggested that delegates return to their respective states and ask state legislators to grant them the right to determine what kind of programs were going to prepare teachers, who would enter those programs, who would be licensed to teach, and who would be considered competent enough and ethical enough to continue to teach... ."

Yes, you read it right. As far back as 1856 the NEA was preparing for HR6, Goals 2000, and who would be licensed to teach. As early as 1932, behavior modification and an experimental model of outcome-based education were already in the works. Educational Marxists such as William H. Kilpatrick and George S. Corents were having a tremendous influence upon NEA thinking. "Conditioning," wrote the NEA, "is therefore a process, which may be employed by the teacher to build up attitudes in the child, and predispose him to the actions, by which these attitudes are expressed" (*Tenth Yearbook, Department of Superintendence*).

By 1934, the NEA attack upon the free enterprise system was clearly evident. A report issued by Willard E. Givens at a session of the Department of Superintendence explained that, "Many drastic changes must be made. A dying *laissez-faire* attitude must be completely destroyed and all of us, including the owners, must be subjected to a large degree of social control. A large section of our discussion group maintains that the credit agencies, the basic industries and utilities cannot be centrally planned and operated under private ownership." That, my friends, is pure, unadulterated socialism. Is it any wonder, then, that the government school textbooks have exhibited a definite socialist bias since the 1930's? To add insult to injury, in 1935, socialist Givens was made NEA Executive Secretary. He ran the whole show until 1952! Need I say more?

Glorifying the New World Order and the Communist revolution, the NEA had this to say in 1937: "The present capitalistic and nationalistic social system has been supplanted in but one place—Russia—and that change was effected by revolution. Hence the verdict of history would seem to indicate that we are likely to have to depend upon revolution for social change of an important and far-reaching character" (*Fifteenth Yearbook, Department of Superintendence*). This is why the public schools are really socialist schools—places of indoctrination and propaganda!

Moving on to 1948, OBE and behavior modification are back in the limelight. The NEA stated, "The school program must include experience designed to tap all the sources that go into producing the desired behavior characteristics of the world-minded American. Actual changes in behavior is the goal, and any modification in behavior entails changes in attitudes" (*Education For International Understanding In American Schools*).

In 1967 the Dean of the UCLA Graduate School of Education, speaking on behalf of the NEA at the inauguration of its Executive Secretary, promoted the insidious OBE design: "The most controversial issues of the twenty-first century will pertain to the ends and means of modifying human behavior and who shall determine them. The first educational question will not be, 'What knowledge is of most worth?' but 'What kinds of human beings do we wish to produce?' The possibilities virtually defy our imagination."

What difference does it make, as far as the NEA is concerned, if children cannot read, write, spell, add, subtract, or divide? As long as the student feels good about himself and is "politically correct" in his thinking, he has been educated.

20/20 Vision

In his writings thirty years ago dealing with American schools, Verne Kaub fearlessly told the truth:

> "So-called and self-styled progressive educators, occupying policy-forming positions within the National Education Association, and its divisions and departments, have not hesitated to use the exact language of the Communist-Socialist movement in describing their social-economic aims, and in urging teachers to indoctrinate the youth of the land for acceptance of socialistic ideology and programs."

Is it any wonder that the *American Legion Magazine* of June 1952 called the NEA

> "one of the strongest forces today in propagandizing for a socialist America.... Some of its performances have been more typical of a captured labor union, complete with goon squads, than a respectable national organization of more than half a million teachers."

The formation, then, of the current secular practices of education was the culmination of a long, patient program, to which the post-World War I breakdown of morals and discipline (a tendency that follows every war, seemingly) was the catalyst that brought the educational "revolt" to fruition.

During this same period there was great growth in the demand for education. After World War II, for instance, the "GI Bill" offered a college education to virtually every returning veteran. The result was a great influx of teachers into the system, created by "production line" techniques without much regard for ability. This fit the pattern of progressive education to a nice degree, because it increased the leveling effect of a system which stifled individual effort and ability.

Progressive education, you see, in its effort to "adjust" the child, decried competition. Its ultimate goal did not permit any measure of achievement such as report cards. Classes were not to be divided into groups according to ability. Time spent was the measure. After the requisite time, a student was advanced whether he merited it or not. Thus ineffectual teachers made no real difference, which helps explain the phenomenon of high school graduates who could not read or do even simple arithmetic, much less bear any resemblance to being "educated" in that classical sense prevalent only a few years earlier.

Today the distraught parent, appalled by this ignorance, finds himself further thwarted by the mechanics of some of the new methods of teaching, such as the "new math." He finds himself in the unenviable position of wanting to help but not being able to, for the simple reason that he cannot figure out what on earth is going on! This, of course, furthers the concept that the sooner a child finds his own niche in his peer group and removes himself from the deleterious influence of home and family, the better.

The "old" education involved three elements: the pupil, the teacher, and the body of knowledge which the teacher was trying to communicate. In other words, the curriculum was standard and required, and the relationship between teacher and pupil was clearly defined. Now, however, if the child does not see fit to study history, or if the teacher thinks he can find a "meaningful lifestyle" without studying grammar, the average child will slither through school with no idea of what he has missed, and no reason to suspect its existence.

It is a characteristic of human beings to scoff at things they do not understand or know. Thus, the pupils jeer not only at traditional values, but also at what, not many years ago, were standard, required subjects, and the teachers join the mockery by making light of the basics of education.

A father, on one of the rare days when the parents are permitted to visit the school, was appalled at the grammar used by his son's math teacher. It was not colloquial or slang; it was just plain bad and inexcusable. He mentioned this to another boy's father, a man loud in his pronouncements about community affairs, and schooling in particular, but the other man's response was, "Oh, well. That may be. But he's the best track coach the school's ever had!"

A teenage girl in junior high school was pleased that her English course for the ensuing year was designated as a study of literature. To her disappointment and her parents' dismay, her entire school year was spent in reading *The Call Of The Wild!* This was the foundation for her knowledge of English literature!

REBUILDING THE WALLS

Not too many years ago, before this age of hyper-specialization, a liberal arts college education was looked on as useful in that it purported to teach the student to think. But no mind, however brilliant, can think and grow if it has nothing to think about. The Bible says, "The fear of the Lord is the beginning of knowledge;" however, "fools despise wisdom and instruction." As Dr. Rushdoony has stated in his book, *The Philosophy Of The Christian Curriculum*, "The struggle for Christian schools is the battle for the survival of biblical faith. The Great Community of Humanism is simply Babylon the Great of Scripture, the great enemy of faith and of Christian man."

May we as Christians learn from the mistakes of the past. Let us rise up and rebuild the walls of education. Let us reconstruct for the glory of King Jesus.

Chapter 2

Parental Reasons for Leaving Public Education

Consider the words of Paul Blanshard, a pioneer in the humanist movement, reflecting upon the objectives and values of public education:

> "I think that the most important factor moving us toward a secular society has been the educational factor. Our schools may not teach Johnny to read properly, but the fact that Johnny is in school until he is sixteen tends to lead towards the elimination of religious superstition. The average American child now acquires a high school education and this militates against Adam and Eve and all the other myths of alleged history.... When I was one of the editors of *The Nation* in the 20's, I wrote an editorial explaining that golf and intelligence were the two primary reasons why men did not attend church; perhaps I would now say golf and a high school diploma."

The expression "public education" is commonly understood to mean education financed by the people through tax money. Public education, however, gets more than money from the public. It gets ideas, goals, values, objectives, direction, beliefs, concepts, and opinions. In short, public education is really an extension of the public and not just an extension of the public's pocketbook. It is in this larger, yet less measurable, aspect of "public education" that we find our greatest concern. Quite frankly, many parents do not share the goals, values, concepts, direction, objectives, and beliefs that characterize the general population of our country today. There is a gap between them and the public in general and it seems to be widening. This is also the case between them and modern society's powerful offspring—public education.

In addition to all of the academic problems noted in Chapter One, a few of the parental reasons for leaving public education are the following, each of which will be discussed in some detail:

1. From their perspective, they believe public education has shifted its emphasis from that of teaching the academic tools to that of shaping a child's worldview. Educators contend that since many children are not being taught values at home, it, therefore, becomes the school's responsibility to do this. Parents who do not deliberately teach values to their children probably will not object if someone else does. But parents who do teach values to their children are concerned about who does the teaching and what system of values is being used.
2. They disagree with the evolutionary concept of origins that is almost uniformly presented to their children in public school textbooks.
3. They disagree with the concept of history and how it is usually interpreted and taught in public schools.
4. They disagree with the concepts that are generally presented to their children regarding human relationships, i.e., social studies. Specifically, they reject the concepts that are presented by most psychology textbooks.
5. They object to the measure or standard of success that is often assumed in the public schools.
6. They disagree with what they have observed to be public education's policy on student discipline.
7. They object to the excessive peer pressure present in most public schools, especially at the junior high level.
8. They object to having their children spend twelve very important years of their lives in the oftentimes sheltered and artificial world of public education.

From Teaching the Basics to Shaping the Child

Reading, writing, arithmetic, bookkeeping, chemistry, physics and typing are tools. Some of these, in fact, are very valuable tools. But like a car in the garage or a rifle on the wall, these tools take on practical value only as they are put into use. Used in a proper way, they are good. They can also be used for evil, however, and when they are, these same tools are harmful. In years gone by, American public education offered the basic academic tools with an emphasis upon the three

Rs. The instruction on how to best use these tools—how to live and think and work—came primarily from the home and the church. But things have changed. The academic tools are still offered, but along with it modern public education, in our opinion, is increasingly giving its own brand of instruction on how to live, think, and work. Public education is in the business of disseminating morals, values, and a comprehensive philosophy of life. Often this occurs in the social sciences, which include family planning and sex education courses. The educators we have spoken to usually do not deny that morals and values are being taught. The typical response seems to be, "More and more students are coming to school these days without any real training in the area of values. If parents don't teach their children values, then the public schools must." On the surface, this sounds innocent enough and even seems commendable. Parents object, however, to the idea that a state institution, which should be separate from the church, should presume to adopt a humanistic worldview and to teach those values to their children.

Parents object even more strongly to the worldview that has become, in recent years, the framework for formulating these values. How a person lives depends upon how that person thinks, or one's worldview. And the worldview that increasingly characterizes today's public education is as far from the historical Christian view as black is from white.

Just in terms of sex education, for example, the government schools in Washington, D.C., were among the first in the nation to institute a kindergarten through 12th grade program of sex education. And the national capital has become the first major U.S. city where the number of babies killed by abortion exceeds the number of live births.

Many people, including many educators themselves, do not know what humanism is, yet the unmistakable worldview of modern public education in this country is *humanism*. From Webster's *Seventh New Collegiate Dictionary*, we find the following as one of the definitions of humanism:

> a doctrine, attitude or way of life centered on human interests or values., esp: a philosophy that asserts the dignity and worth of man and his capacity for self-realization through reason and that often rejects supernaturalism.

Parents believe that consciously or unconsciously public schools have become seminaries for the religion of humanism. One of the first and most important areas in which this is evident is the teaching of origins.

THE EVOLUTIONARY VIEW OF ORIGINS: THE MYTH THAT THE WORLD MADE ITSELF

The Bible insists that the end of all being—the purpose of existence—is the glory of the Creator by whom and for whom all things are made. In contrast, humanism and our public school textbooks, explicitly or implicitly, teach that there is no Creator, that everything evolved unto present day complexity and order through a strange twist of fate through long eons of time, and that the end of all being is the happiness and progress of *man*. Beginning with biology and extending into the social sciences, students are being trained to believe that existence—their own and everything about them—is the product of chance. Almost without exception, the biology and social science textbooks currently used in the pubic classrooms exclusively teach the evolutionary time/chance framework. As a result, young minds are often left with the understanding that the only academically acceptable explanation of origins is the evolutionary one.

While many parents make their children aware of the theory of evolution when they know the truth of God's word, they object to the teaching that the evolutionary theory of origins is the scientific explanation of origins. In their opinion, it is neither scientific nor true. Concerning the evolutionary worldview, they suggest that the motivation for promoting it lies solely in its underlying philosophical assumption of materialism—there is no Creator. If the existence of the Creator is precluded before the discussion begins, then some form of evolution has to be true regardless of the facts that disprove it. This is what makes the theory of evolution a blind religion; it is true regardless of how much evidence is against it. It is put into the academic ring by itself and declared to be the winner—without a contest. When the theory of evolution began, it was challenged. But evolutionists requested more time to check out the fossil record, to refine their serology tests, to trace down all the vestigial organs, to compare anatomies and search for favorable mutations, to polish up the argument for embryonic recapitulation, and to complete the description of the "simple" cell. The novelty and challenge of exploring some relatively new concepts, along with a good deal of personal bias, swept Darwin's theories past the initial challengers right up to the front of the class. A hundred years later, this theory which has been revised many times is still hunting for pegs to hang on.

The fossil record is an embarrassment because after a century of intensive searching the critical links are still in the imagination. Serology tests have failed and the 'vestigial' organs have all but disappeared as continued research reveals heretofore unknown functions for supposedly useless organs. Comparative anatomy, with its familiar evolutionary tree, is based on the theory to begin with and thus can prove nothing. The search for favorable mutations has proved futile. What has been discovered is a relatively stable gene machinery with a large but limited gene bank and occasional mutations, which are harmful to the population. The argument for embryonic recapitulation is generally discredited by all but school textbook writers. The theory of the evolution of the modern horse has fallen upon hard times, relying, in our opinion, more upon good artists and youthful memories for support than upon solid evidence.

Besides not being able in a hundred years to establish the theory any better than when Darwin first proposed it, the search for proof itself has raised some unexpected problems. The simple cell has proved itself staggeringly complex. Once it was thought that the big problem was in getting from the amoeba to the man. Now going from amoeba to man is but the final stage of the journey. The real difficulty is in getting non-living, random materials together to form living cells.

The geologic time chart with its millions and billions of years, an essential feature of the evolutionary theory, has been brought into serious question by the discovery of human-like footprints, mingled with brontosaurus tracks, in the Paluxy River bed in Glen Rose, Texas. Furthermore, with the advent of computers, the theory of evolution can no longer hide behind astronomical numbers because now the probability factors can actually be computed. The odds that something may accidentally synthesize itself can be determined, as well as the odds toward dissolution (the reverse of synthesis), and the computers are saying, "No." Adding more time to the evolutionary time chart won't help because the more time you allow for something to accidentally synthesize itself, the more time you allow for dissolution (the opposite of synthesis) to occur. The dissolution factors of non-living, unprogrammed, random molecules are far greater than any trend toward form and order. Except for an abundance of colorful illustrations and speculations, the general theory of evolution is destitute.

Parents do not want their children to be given academically and biblically false instruction when it comes to such an important subject as origins, because our understanding of how we got here has direct bearing on what we are here for, and how we should live while we are here.

THE HUMANISTIC VS. THE CHRISTIAN INTERPRETATION OF HISTORY

Another important area of difference between the Christian worldview and the humanistic worldview that is taught in public schools has to do with history—both the basic concept of history and also the interpretation of history. The facts of history cannot be changed, but how they are interpreted, analyzed, and taught depends upon the historian and the historian's worldview. It does not take a very astute person to realize how those with different worldviews look at history in different ways.

One major area of difference between the historic Christian viewpoint and the humanistic view found in most history textbooks used in public schools has to do with the destiny of human history. Is history going somewhere or is it not? Is there a divine course to human history as the Bible teaches, or is it rather a chance affair? If the Creator has destined the course of human history and has revealed His plans to us, then we ought to submit our thinking and our lives to be a part of His purpose. If, on the other hand, history is a chance affair, then the recent evolution of the human intellect impels us to take the matter into our own hands and forge on ahead as best we can. How we look at life depends to a great extent upon our concept of history. Christian parents believe history is going somewhere, that there is a divine purpose in human history. This is not what is being taught in the public schools.

Besides holding a strikingly different concept of history than that of the public schools, many parents view historical events differently than most textbook writers. The great historical events of the past, from the Christian viewpoint, must include creation, the space-time fall of man into moral guilt, the great flood, the giving of the law to the ancient Hebrew nation, the life of John the Baptist, the birth, death, and resurrection of Jesus Christ, the history of the early Christian church, and the Reformation in northern Europe.

What do children learn from public school textbooks? Instead of the historical creation, they are taught evolution and the "myth" of creation. Instead of the historical fall of man into guilt and the rebellion against the Creator, they are taught that man initially started as a lowly, groveling creature that has since ascended the evolutionary ladder. Instead of the monumental, catastrophic, historical flood, they are taught a uniformitarian concept—that history has been uninterrupted by violent catastrophes. Instead of an historical revelation of the laws of God to the nation of Israel, they are taught that there is no divine revelation and there are no moral absolutes, that morality is a matter of human invention and social contract. They are taught more about the Roman Empire and the Caesars than about John the Baptist, of whom it was recorded that there had not, at that time at least, risen a greater person than he.

The very greatest One of all, the One whose sandals John the Baptist felt unworthy to loosen, the Christ whose birth divides recorded time in two, is given only passing mention. No mention is made of the early Christian church; very little is said about the Reformation. What does receive attention is the Renaissance—the rebirth of humanistic man! Many parents have no objection to informing their children about evolution, the Roman Empire and the Caesars, or about the Renaissance, but they want these things to be presented to their children in such a way that they will understand the utter weakness and poverty of the humanistic worldview, and the truth and certainty of historical Christianity.

THE MODERN HUMANISTIC SOCIAL SCIENCES

"Social Studies" or the "Social Sciences" are the general courses in school which teach us how to relate to ourselves and others. One of the big reasons why parents are leaving the public schools is because the social studies courses, including modern psychology and education, are dominated by the thinking of Sigmund Freud, B. F. Skinner, John Dewey, and other humanistic thinkers.

Christian parents recognize the influence that our environment can have upon them. They can see why humanistic thinkers would feel a need to monitor and modify society. But because they do not work from the humanist framework in their thinking, they utterly reject the basic teaching that comes out of most social studies textbooks used in the public schools. They believe in the dignity of man and the significance of the individual—not as humanists, who can do so only through irrational assertion—but on the basis that they were created in the image of the Creator (Genesis 1:27). Rejecting the idea of human autonomy (absolute freedom) as well as environmental determinism, the Bible teaches that man is a slave of sin and under the curse and judgment of God. He is thereby subject to adversity from his environment as well as corruption and injustice in society. God created man with freedom to choose, but because of his bondage to sin he can never be free unless the Son sets him truly free by saving faith. There are universal moral standards set down by the Creator in the Ten Commandments and true moral guilt (not just guilt feeling) when these standards are violated. They believe in recognition of guilt, honest confession of guilt to those offended, including the Creator, and restitution to injured parties, whenever possible.

THE BIBLICAL VS. THE HUMANISTIC MEASURE OF SUCCESS

There are people who see little relationship between one's worldview and real life. But make no mistake, abstract worldviews have concrete implications. Parents do not think it is too strong a statement to say that if a child grows up embracing and practicing the humanistic worldview which has become the hallmark of modern education, he would bear little, if any, resemblance to the person he would have become if he had embraced the Christian worldview. There is no better place to begin in showing that different worldviews actually do make different people than in the area of success.

Throughout life a person is encouraged to be successful. Children hear it from their parents; they hear it from their teachers; they hear it from their counselors. When they get a job, they hear it from their boss, and when they eventually own the business, they hear it at business conventions. It is important to be successful. That is why it is of paramount importance to know what constitutes true success. What is the measure of success?

The Christian worldview measures success by how well a person does the Creator's will on earth. It should go without saying that if we are made by the Creator, then our purpose here is to do what the Creator wants us to do. What He wants us to do—His will for us—is to trust Him, enjoy Him, and honor Him by practicing what is right and honorable in our everyday lives. More specifically, our Christian worldview motivates us to look to the Bible for its view of success.

THE LAW OF GOD AND SUCCESS

True success is clearly revealed to us in Scripture when God gave his law to Moses on Mt. Sinai. He said, "This book of the law shall not depart from your mouth, but you shall meditate on it day and night, so that you may be careful to do according to all that is written in it; for then you will make your way prosperous, and then you will have success" (Joshua 1:8). Only God can define success for us. When the public schools removed God's law as the standard of right and wrong, we lost the basis of the success of earlier generations.

The foundation of success is found in the summary of the law, "Thou shalt love the Lord thy God with all thy heart, and with all thy soul, and with all thy mind. This is the first and great commandment. And the second is like unto it: Thou shalt love thy neighbor as thyself. On these two commandments hang all the law and the prophets." A person is truly successful if he loves God and people with genuine love; if he seeks to honor others rather than seeking self-honor (Rom. 12:9-10; Phil. 2:3-4). In whatever he does, he works as unto the Lord and not for man (Col. 3:23). He becomes a servant of others (Mark 10:42-

44). He is not conceited, but willing to associate with people of low status and does not show favoritism to the rich and influential (Rom. 12:16; James 2:1-4). Above all he lives to promote God's kingdom and prepares himself spiritually for conflict with the supernatural evil powers (Eph. 6:10-18). Therefore he strives to have a clear conscience before both God and man (Acts 24:16).

1st Commandment:
Thou Shalt Have No Other Gods Before Me

A person is successful if he does not divide his allegiance between God and the world system. His allegiance is only to God. Participation and involvement in the world system, when such occurs, would be part of his service and commitment to God. If success means hungering and thirsting for righteousness and ordering our lives in the pursuit of it, then how will our children grow up to be successful when, instead of teaching that God's absolutes of good and evil are revealed to us all and that we should embrace the good and reject the evil, public school textbooks teach that there are no moral absolutes, that we make the rules as we go, based upon social desire or expediency? Someone is successful if he hungers and thirsts for righteousness; if he hates what is evil and clings to what is good; if he rejoices in the truth; if he does not love the world system with its sinful cravings, the lusts of the eyes, and its pride in material possessions (Matt. 5:6; Rom. 12:9; 1 Cor. 13:6; 1 John 2:15-16). He is successful because he does not allow himself to be pushed into a cultural mold, but is renewed in his own thinking on subjects by reviewing God's word so as to understand how God thinks about things (Rom. 12:1-2; Eph. 4:17-24).

2nd Commandment:
Thou Shalt Not Make Unto Thee Any Graven Image

If success means worshiping and serving the infinite, personal Creator, then how will our children grow up to be successful when modern public education has become infiltrated with materials that, directly or indirectly, teach that there is no Creator? If success is preparing for spiritual conflict with the supernatural powers of evil by using the Word of God and prayer, how can my children be successful when modern public education, by teaching scientific positivism, often dismisses the existence of God altogether? A person is truly successful if he worships the Lord his God and serves Him only; if he rejoices in Him and praises Him; if he acknowledges God in his thinking as sovereign Lord and ruler of his life (Matt. 4:10; Phil. 4:4; 1 Pet. 3:15; Heb. 13:5). He is successful as he devotes himself to prayer (Rom. 12:1-2, Col. 4:2; 1 Tim 2:1-2). He does not practice his religion for public recognition and does not recognize or willingly accept religious titles (Matt. 6:1-18; Matt. 23:5-10; Mark 12:38-40). He is not taken captive through the idols of our age, the hollow and deceptive philosophies which depend on human tradition and the basic principles of the evil world system (Col. 2:8).

3RD COMMANDMENT:
THOU SHALT NOT TAKE THE NAME OF THE LORD THY GOD IN VAIN

True success involves a proper understanding of who God is and how we should think about Him according to His word. This is expressed in our words. We must talk about God from a proper theology that is carefully derived from the Bible. A successful person controls his tongue and does not allow unwholesome talk to come out of his mouth, but speaks only what is helpful for building up others. He does not engage in obscenity, foolish talk, or coarse joking, and he avoids godless chatter by speaking graciously and wisely (Eph. 4:29; Col. 4:6; 2 Tim. 2:16; Eph. 5:4).

4TH COMMANDMENT:
REMEMBER THE SABBATH DAY, TO KEEP IT HOLY

While our age is often caught between the two poles of overwork and laziness, the Bible teaches us the necessity of diligence for success. "Poor is he who works with a negligent hand, but the hand of the diligent makes rich" (Proverbs 10:4). This is the basis of the Protestant or biblical work ethic. Because it is not being taught in the public schools, we have seen a continual decline in American productivity and our ability to excel in a world market. Instead, the humanistic view is that work is either an evil to be avoided or purely a means of the attainment of material wealth. The biblical view of work involves laboring for six days and resting on the seventh, after God's example in creation. Our children are taught by this that life's sole purpose is not for work and obtaining money, but that all things exist for God's glory and that our worship and enjoyment of Him should be the goal of our work. Thus we make the Lord's day special as a time of worship and rest. Thereby we are refreshed for our work week in both body and spirit, and are reminded of the eternal rest that awaits us in heaven.

5TH COMMANDMENT: HONOR THY FATHER AND THY MOTHER

Success includes developing a proper relationship with those in authority over us, or with those under our authority in the home, at work, and in the state. A person is successful if he obeys the government in all that is honorable (Rom. 13:1-7; Tit. 3:1-2; 1 Pet. 2:13). Such a person is not intimidated by human authority when human government is opposed to God's laws (Acts 5:29).

In the workplace he serves his boss with sincerity of heart and does honest work. He does not talk back or steal from his employer in terms of time or possessions, but shows that he can be fully trusted (Eph. 6:5-8; Col. 3:22; Titus 2:9-10). In the same way a manager is successful when he treats his employees or servants with fairness and kindness (Eph. 6:9; Col. 4:1).

In the family a person is successful if he obeys and honors his parents (Eph. 6:2). A wife is successful if she loves and respects her husband and submits to him. When she is faithful, pure, and busy at home she makes herself beautiful, with a gentle and quiet spirit (Eph. 5:22-23; 1 Tim. 2:11-12; Tit. 2:4-5; 1 Pet. 3:1-4). A father is successful if he does not exasperate his children, but brings them up in the training and instruction of the Lord (Eph. 6:4; Col. 3:21).

6th Commandment: Thou shalt not kill

A biblical view of success involves a promotion of the sanctity of life and a concern for the life of our neighbor. We find a sharp contrast between the biblical ethic of being merciful and kind, and the basic framework of modern public education, which is built upon the 'survival of the fittest' concept. What place does mercy and kindness have in a classroom that teaches tooth and claw survival? Not all students will be as inconsistent as some text materials, which try to put a benevolent face on their humanistic-evolutionary worldview. This certainly explains why there is increasing violence in public schools.

A successful person is merciful (Matt. 5:7), a peacemaker that tries to live at peace with everyone (Matt. 5:9; Rom. 12:18). He loves his enemies and prays for those who persecute him, and does not return evil for evil in an attempt to get even; he does not seek revenge (Matt. 5:44; Rom. 12:17; Rom. 12:10). He does not get into heated, angry quarrels and arguments, and avoids foolish and stupid arguments (Rom. 13:13; 2 Tim. 2:16, 23-24). He is kind and compassionate and forgives others (Eph. 4:32; Col. 3:12-13). He also confesses his sins to those whom he has offended (James 5:16).

7th Commandment: Thou shalt not commit adultery

God's way of success means following his purpose for men and women in respect to marriage. If being pure in thought and deed is part of a successful life, how shall our children be successful when modern public education not only refuses to oppose the flood of immorality which is sweeping the campuses, but actually condones such activity? At the heart of our educational system is a worldview which promotes sexual liberation. The Christian worldview renounces fornication, adultery, and homosexual acts. Much of modern education, however, teaches that these practices are acceptable, right, and beautiful between *responsible* people. Is it strange, then, that Christian parents are concerned about the marriage and sex education courses that have sprung up in many of the secondary schools throughout the country?

A person is truly successful if he is pure in thought and deed; if he does not think about adultery nor defile himself with evil thoughts, sexual immorality, lewdness, orgies, prostitution, and homosexual acts (Matt. 5:8,27-28; Mark 7:20-23; Rom. 1:24-31; Rom. 13:13; 1 Cor. 6:9; Gal. 5:19-21; Col. 3:5; 1 Pet. 4:3). He honors his marriage vows, loves and cherishes his wife and cares for her, just as he would for himself. He is not unfaithful to her even in his own thought-life. He is not harsh with her; is considerate and treats her with respect (Matt. 19:3-9; Matt. 5:27; Eph. 5:25-28; Col. 3:19; Heb. 13:4; 1 Pet. 3:7). Both men and women will dress modestly and decently (1 Tim. 2:9-10). The public schools know nothing of this measure of success.

8TH COMMANDMENT: THOU SHALT NOT STEAL

If success results from doing a job or pursuing a vocation that is actually doing someone good, will any children turn out successful when they are taught in the schools that a good job is primarily one that is enjoyable, and that pulls down a good salary? I want my children to grow up understanding that in addition to being enjoyable and financially profitable, a job, to be good, must be one that helps people by providing a good service or by manufacturing a good product. We cannot be unmindful of wages and salaries, but there are more important considerations than the dollar bill.

A person is successful if he devotes himself to honest, wholesome work in order that he may provide for his own and not lead an idle or unproductive life (Titus 3:14; 1 Thess. 4:11-12; 2 Thess. 3:11-12). Such a person does not practice theft, murder, greed, malice, deceit, envy, and slander to get ahead. Such a person does not allow debts to remain unpaid (Rom. 13:8). And instead of thinking only about what he can get from others, he practices hospitality (Rom. 12:13; Heb. 13:1) and is a friend of strangers.

9TH COMMANDMENT: THOU SHALT NOT BEAR FALSE WITNESS AGAINST THY NEIGHBOR

A person is successful if he puts away falsehood and speaks truthfully with his neighbor (Eph. 4:25). Instead of deceit, treachery, and hypocrisy, he practices honesty and faithfulness. He promotes truth between people, and promotes the truth of the Scriptures always. He does not twist the truth to his own advantage, but honors God as the God of truth. He is a person of his word and becomes the type of person that can be depended upon in various relationships in family and at work. The public schools, however, would promote pragmatism—that any action can be justified if it has a "good" end. This philosophy does not honor the sanctity of truth because it will not honor the God of truth, whose Word is the truth.

10TH COMMANDMENT: THOU SHALT NOT COVET

If success is being content with food, shelter, and clothing and not being preoccupied with material possessions and the love of money, how then can public education properly train our children when it is both parent and offspring of a society inflamed with desire to accumulate possessions? Since public education reflects so much of our materialistically-oriented society, how can it do anything but perpetuate the trend unless it ceased being 'public'? Until that happens, our children will breathe, year after year, the infected atmosphere which, when analyzed and verbalized, comes out something like this: "Work hard at your studies so that you can go to college, so you can get a good job, so you can earn a lot of money, so you can buy a car, a boat, and a house in the suburbs."

A person is truly successful if he is not preoccupied with material possessions and does not live to accumulate them, but keeps his life free from love for money, being content with whatever God gives (Matt. 6:19-33; Heb. 13:5; 1 Tim. 6:6-10). He is not worried about anything, but trusts in God, making his requests known to Him with thanksgiving (Phil. 4:6). He gives and loans as able to those in need. He is concerned for widows and orphans in their distress, is generous and willing to share (Matt. 5:42; 1 Tim. 6:17-19; Rom. 12:13; James 1:27). All in all he is thankful for the portion God has given to him and expresses his thankfulness to God (Eph. 5:4, 20; Heb. 13:15).

The Bible clearly shows what constitutes success. After considering the true nature of success from the Christian perspective, none who know what characterizes modern public education will fail to see how mutually exclusive the two viewpoints are in this supremely important area.

Public Education and Discipline

Parents believe that children are to be trained and taught the way they should go and that disobedient, rebellious attitudes in children are to be handled with loving, yet firm, discipline. Modern public education, in general, frowns upon correcting a child's behavioral and emotional activity lest the child receive psychological trauma. Indeed, teachers are forbidden to administer physical discipline. Between modern psychology and the law, parents believe that their children are not likely to receive the discipline they so often need.

In addition to this, modern education has adopted the concept that children should be allowed to progress at their own speed. Those teachers who still remember the days of strict grading, rigid class requirements, and who have seen children respond to such teaching, do not always drop the pressure to perform even though the system now features the go-at-your-own-speed philosophy.

Younger teachers, however, who are entering the ranks without prior experience may underestimate just how fast an average second or third grader, for instance, can learn if there is some wisely applied pressure put upon him. Children will not make top progress either emotionally or academically without wise incentives, strict discipline, and carefully-chosen ultimatum deadlines. Furthermore, the hard, cold world of jobs and business competition which they enter upon graduation is not going to tolerate a person who goes at his own speed. It is, "Performance, or else." Consequently, parents may be cheating and misleading their children if they teach them to progress at their own speed.

Excessive Peer Pressure and an Artificial World

A non-academic feature about modern public education that concerns us is the influence of our children's peers upon our children. Not all peer pressure is bad. Nevertheless, negative peer pressure has destroyed many young people, and parents want to avoid this if at all possible.

Children must learn to get along with other people, including their peers. Parents do not want them to live a sheltered life and be unable to relate to others. They want them to know what goes on in the world around them. In a good sense, they want their children to be more contemporary than others their age. But what they don't want is to have them confronted by the excessive peer pressure that seems to be typical of most public schools, especially at the junior high level.

In some ways, it seems to a growing number of parents that the segment of modern society which we call the public school system is almost a world unto itself. It is a world of people who have spent most of their lives within the world of public education, many of whom see it as a grand opportunity to experiment in social engineering. Being specialized is important, but it can lead to an exclusiveness which isolates it from the real world. They feel that, to a degree, this has happened. It is a world where sports and games can easily consume a person's time and thinking. Those who contend that parents are unwisely sheltering their children by taking them out of the public school system must realize that the argument goes both ways. If there is sheltering to be done, they prefer to shelter their children from the sheltered and artificial world of public education.

Chapter 3

A Time for Change

Since 1989, Christian Liberty Academy School System has been working in the former Soviet Union helping to establish Christian schools. We played a major role in the organizing of the very first Christian school in Russia since the Communist Revolution in 1918. It began in 1989 in Moscow.

Some years ago, I was invited to Moscow to lecture at a conference sponsored by Moscow's educational leadership—both public and private school. The location was the former Communist Party headquarters in Moscow. The theme of my lectures was this: an educational program without Christ and a Christian philosophy of education is a recipe for disaster.

Conference participants asked questions for several hours. They were very interested. The press was also in attendance, both TV, radio and the print media, and my message, at least in part, was broadcast over Moscow TV.

As I discussed the moral and educational potential of Christian schools, I pointed out that we must first understand the moral and educational decline in America. The remainder of this chapter are excerpts from my Russian remarks:

What we see morally in America, for example, among the general population, we also see clearly reflected in her schools. Crime is becoming more and more widespread throughout American society. And likewise violence, vandalism, and drugs in the nation's public schools are approaching epidemic proportions.

Within recent years, school-related homicides have increased by 18 percent. Rapes and attempted rapes within the schools have increased by 40 percent. Assaults on students and teachers have also taken a tremendous jump—over 75 percent. Robberies are up 37 percent, and drug and alcohol offenses on school property have increased by 38 percent. The National Congress of Parents and Teachers has warned, "The increasing intensity and frequency of violence and vandalism in the schools threatens serious disruption of the educational process." Not only, therefore, are there the problems of declining academic performance (Chapter 1) and a distorted worldview (Chapter 2), but crime and drugs within the schools are catastrophic.

We believe the solution is a simple one—to prepare each student to glorify God, to enjoy Him, and to serve Him in a chosen calling. The students within our educational system attend many different churches: Baptist, Roman Catholic, Lutheran, Presbyterian, Pentecostal, Evangelical Free, and many others. We do not instruct them toward a particular denomination. Rather, we seek to emphasize the fact that "The fear of the Lord is the beginning of knowledge" (Proverbs 1:7).

Our Christian education is not a curriculum with the Bible added to it. Rather, the inspired word of God governs and informs every subject in our curriculum.

Average students who have been taught by way of our Christian program are scoring anywhere from one and a half to three years above the national averages in reading, spelling, math, and other basic skills. Besides the scholastic achievements, students have learned:

- **In Science**—that they are studying God's laws for the universe.
- **In Math**—God's constancy in a world of apparent flux.
- **In History**—God's plan for the ages and the redemption of His people.
- **In Language**—to communicate truth to others.
- **In Government**—that all true government is ordained of God for certain specific and limited purposes.
- **In Literature**—to test other writers by Christian standards.
- **In Economics**—basic principles proceeding from an orderly God.

The greater the influence of this constructive philosophy upon a system of education, the greater the moral and academic potential and benefits to that system of education.

There are many parallels between America in the seventeenth, eighteenth, and nineteenth centuries and Russia today. Your new education policies are being constructed.

If you choose to look to America, may it be the America of the past and not the present. A Christian philosophy of education that relates to every area of life is the philosophical and theological foundation you want. Having worked within the public school system, as well as the private and Christian school system for over 30 years, please believe me when I tell you that the American public school system is not the model for Russia to follow.

Our public schools have been weighed in the balance. They have been found wanting. The secularization of education is a recipe for educational disaster. In the Scriptures we read, "Whatsoever a man soweth, that shall he also reap" (Gal 6:7). In America, we are reaping a whirlwind.

I believe that even if the Russian government, or any other government, was successful in mandating an academically, doctrinally, and morally perfect educational program, that very mandate, in and of itself, would be a violation of Scriptural precepts. Our children are not the wards of the government. Education is not a proper function of civil government. It is the parents, and not the state, whom God has commanded to train up a child. Education belongs in the home or in the school of the parents' choosing. It does not belong in the tax-fed, socialistic, and increasingly anti-God government schools.

Yes, "the fear of the Lord is the beginning of wisdom, and the knowledge of the Holy One is understanding" (Prov 9:10). Remember this—what shall it profit a man if he gain the whole world ... and yet lose his children to the humanists. May God, by His sovereign grace, enable you to be faithful.

A Choice Program In Home Schooling

from *Christian Liberty Academy School System* (**CLASS**)

1 THE CLASS ADMINISTRATION PLAN	**2** THE FAMILY ADMINISTRATION PLAN
For accountability, detailed structure and guidance.	For maximum flexibility, control of workload and schedule.
WE grade your student's tests, issue report cards four times a year, keep your records for you, and issue the diplomas.	YOU grade your student's tests, issue your own report cards, keep your own records, and issue your own diplomas.

BOTH PLANS INCLUDE

- Grades Kindergarten through Twelve
- Textbooks Selected from 25 Different Publishers
- Basic Skills Testing (Grades 2—12)
- Custom Designed Curriculum
- Complete Curriculum Supplied (books, tests, keys, etc.)
- Practical Curriculum Materials (which include a 220 page handbook)
- High School Electives
- School Records Maintenance Instructions and Forms (for Family Administration Plan enrollments)

Home school your children inexpensively with the nationally recognized *Christian Liberty Academy School System* program. Thousands of students in 50 states and more than 50 foreign countries.

For further information, write or phone for your free Information Packet:

Christian Liberty Academy School System
502 West Euclid Avenue
Arlington Heights, IL 60004 **(800) 348-0899**

BUILD YOUR CHRISTIAN SCHOOL CURRICULUM

with DISCOUNT BOOKS
from *Christian Liberty Press*

A FULL LINE OF SUBJECTS...

- PHONICS
- READING
- HANDWRITING
- SPELLING
- GRAMMAR
- MATHEMATICS
- BIBLE
- CHRISTIAN BIOGRAPHIES
- HISTORY
- SCIENCE
- GOVERNMENT
- ECONOMICS

...FROM KINDERGARTEN THROUGH 12TH GRADE
AT DISCOUNT PRICES!!!

Featuring books from *Christian Liberty Press* plus selected titles from A Beka, Bob Jones, Christian Schools International, Modern Curriculum Press, and several other publishers.

**FOR YOUR FREE CATALOG:
PHONE (800) 832-2741**

or you may write:

Christian Liberty Press
502 West Euclid Avenue
Arlington Heights, IL 60004
www.christianlibertypress.com

NOTES

NOTES

NOTES

NOTES